HEMP MACRAMÉ

HEMP MACRAMÉ

Jenny Townley

LARK

New York

LARK
New York

An Imprint of Sterling Publishing
1166 Avenue of the Americas
New York, NY 10036

ISBN 978-1-4547-0949-7

Distributed in Canada by Sterling Publishing Co., Inc.
c/o Canadian Manda Group, 664 Annette Street
Toronto, Ontario, Canada M6S 2C8

For information about custom editions, specials sales, and premium and corporate purchase, please contact Sterling Special Sales at 800-805-5489 or specialsales@sterlingpublishing.com

Manufactured in Hong Kong

2 4 6 8 10 9 7 5 3 1

CONTENTS

INTRODUCTION

I was first inspired to learn about micro-macramé when I spotted some fabulous creations and pieces of work on the internet, and wondered how on earth they were made. I did not have a clue how this was done at the time, so I bought some books about knots and basically taught myself through practicing. Looking back, I must admit my first attempts were pretty dismal, but I did choose quite a hard pattern and a difficult knot to start with (diagonal double half hitch knots). I kept on practicing and after several attempts I was getting pretty pleased with the end result.

In the past I used to create egyptian-style jewelry, but even though I still love this look and the mystery behind it all, it appeared to be a very small niche market. My adventurous spirit took over and prompted me to experiment more with colors and knots, and micro-macramé in particular.

I was also especially keen to work with hemp. I love the idea of it being a natural organic product with its own special feel and look. Being a beach lover, I particularly like to create projects in blues, turquoise, and aquas, and blending them with natural hemp reminds me of clear seawater and sandy beaches. I also love the idea that most of the knots were devised by sailors—and this makes me feel even closer to the sea when I am working with macramé.

I am also so pleased that it's possible to purchase hemp in several different shades and not just its natural color. Hemp also comes in several different thicknesses, too—this means both you and I can experiment even more.

I find it really inspiring to try out new colors and macramé textures and mix them around. It's quite amazing how two theoretically identical bracelets can look so different just by changing the color and shades of the beads, or cords, or even just by changing a charm or button. By mixing and swapping textures and colors you can create an endless amount of variations when using this wonderful craft.

For me, working with hemp and macramé boils down to being historic, romantic, natural, and most of all, handmade!

ESSENTIAL SUPPLIES

Split ring

Made from metal and easily opened with pliers. A split ring is sturdier than a jump ring and less likely to distort, so it's particularly good for charms. The split ring is mainly used to start a project—almost a double ring, it is less likely to open and allow the cords to slip through the gap than with a jump ring.

Jump ring

Round or oval in shape, jump rings can be opened and closed with flat-nose pliers. They are used to attach or link items. The smaller rings are less likely to pull open than the larger rings. When opening do not prize apart, but push the ring ends forward and back to avoid weakening the jump ring.

Closed jump ring

This has no break in the ring so cannot open. It is a good alternative to the split ring.

End clasp/Cord ends

Used to finish cords, they are closed with pliers.

Ribbon clamp

Ideal for covering the raw end of a ribbon, they can also be used to finish braids or cords. These are secured with pliers. Press firmly but gently, otherwise the clamp could be damaged.

Lobster claw

A spring closure attached with a jump ring to a fastening: suitable for bracelets and necklaces.

Beads

Today, there is a huge choice of beads in any number of sizes, shapes, and finishes. When selecting beads, the key aspect is to ensure that the hole size for the cord is the correct measurement—this way the bead will easily slide onto the hemp. Know how many strands you will be putting together as this may help with your choices. To avoid problems, take a sample of the hemp with you when buying to ensure you get the right size.

Pliers

I like to use flat-nose pliers, I find them ideal for all the tasks in the coming projects. There are, of course, a variety of pliers on the market. If you don't already have a pair, choose one you find comfortable to use—ideally with a flat edge.

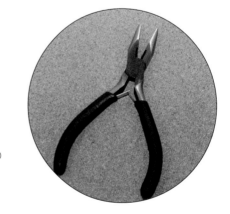

TECHNIQUES

ATTACHING A RIBBON CLAMP

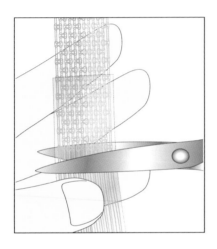

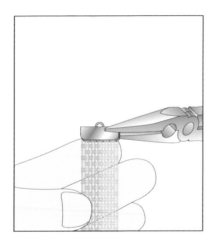

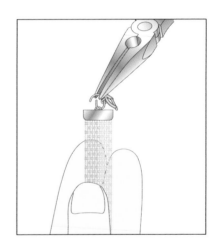

Step #1: Knot your project until it has reached the required length. Pull the loose ends taut and place some transparent adhesive tape on both sides: this will keep the cords straight and prevent any knots from unraveling. Cut the cords quite close to the last row of knots.

Step #2: Place the ribbon clamp over the ends and crimp the clamp closed with pliers. Do this very gently but firmly, to ensure no damage to the clamp. Peel off the tape carefully.

Step #3: Add the jump ring by opening the ring with pliers. Slip the jump ring onto the metal loop on the ribbon clamp; add the lobster claw onto the ring, and then close the ring firmly with the pliers.

TECHNIQUES

ATTACHING AN END CLAMP

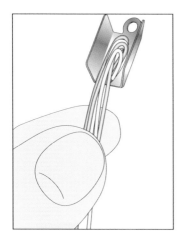

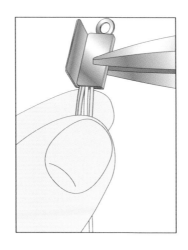

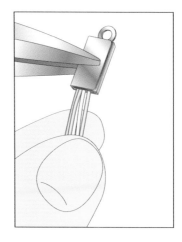

Step #1: Loop your cords to form a neat end and place inside the end clamp. Add a drop of superglue for a secure fit, but do take care not to get any on your fingers.

Step #2: Taking your pliers, bend one side over the cords and clamp securely to close. Put even pressure across the length of the clamp.

Step #3: Repeat with the second side of the clamp, folding this over the first side completely. Again clamp securely to close and ensure that the pressure is even. The end clamp is now in place.

EAR WIRES

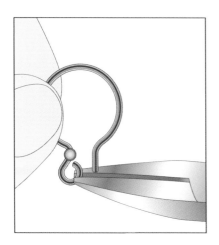

Step #1: Using your pliers, open the ear wire, making sure you pull the wire towards you.

Step #2: Slide your earring, using the loop, onto the ear wire.

Step #3: Close the open side of the loop back, pushing away from you until the loop is securely closed. The earring is now complete.

KNOTS

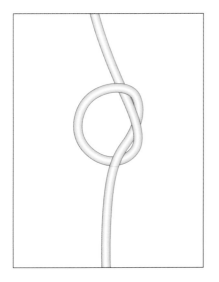

OVERHAND KNOT

This is the basic knot that most people know and mastered when learning how to tie shoelaces. Simply form a loop, pass the tail end through, and then tighten to form the overhand knot.

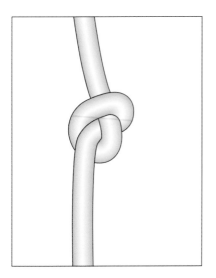

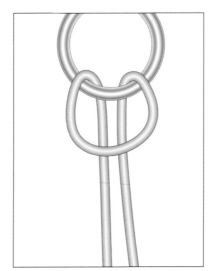

LARKS HEAD KNOT

I use this as my starting knot for most projects. Fold the cords so that they are even in length, loop the cord around the split ring or object being used. Pull the tails through the loop to tighten.

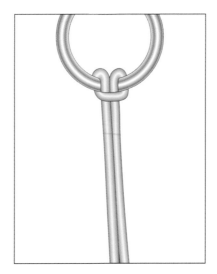

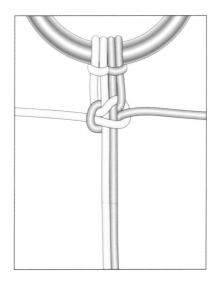

SQUARE KNOT

This is a decorative knot and widely used in macramé. There are two ways to do it (as shown on the following pages): practice both and work with which feels more natural.

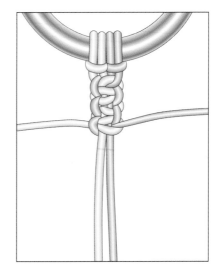

SQUARE KNOT: VERSION 1

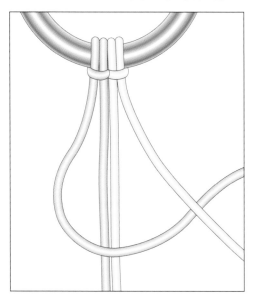

Step #1: Begin with two larks head knots next to each other. Take the far left cord across the center and under the far right cord.

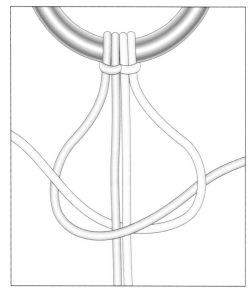

Step #2: Take the far right cord under the center two cords, come up through the loop, and pass over the top of the far left cord.

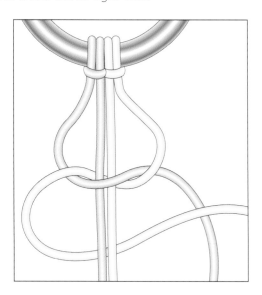

Step #3: Take the left cord under the center cords and over the far right cord.

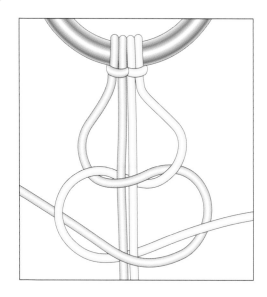

Step #4: Now take the right cord over the center cords, down through the loop created on the left-hand side, and under the far left cord. Pull to tighten and complete.

SQUARE KNOT: VERSION 2

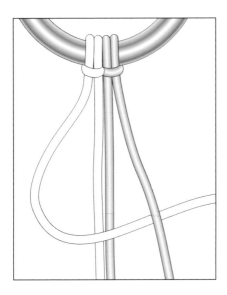

Step #1: Again, begin with two larks head knots. Take the far left cord and run over the center two cords and under the far right cord.

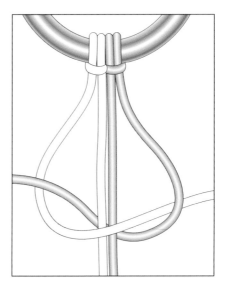

Step #2: Take the far right cord and run under the center two cords, up into the loop and over the top of the far right cord.

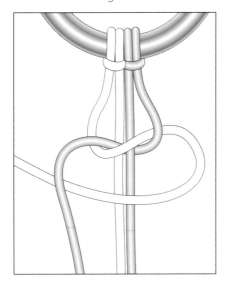

Step #3: Take up the slack so making the top knot tighter. Take the right cord over the center and under the left cord.

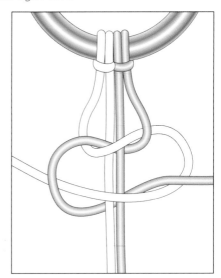

Step #4: Take the left cord under the center two cords, and come up through the loop and over the far right cord. Tighten to close.

ALTERNATING SQUARE KNOT

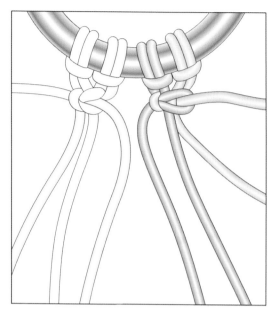

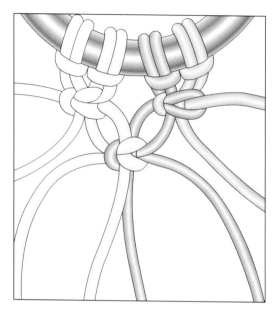

Step #1: Attach cords using a larks head knot. Then tie a square knot with the two left cords (blue and white). Tie a second square knot using the two right cords (purple and pink).

Step #2: Tie a square knot using the two middle pairs of cords (blue and purple) to form a knot in the center of the work.

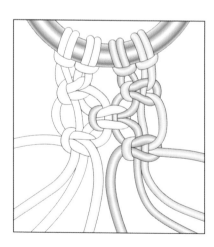

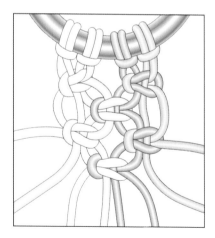

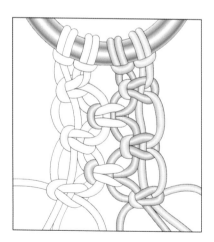

Step #3: Repeat Step 1 using the two far left cords (blue and white) to create a square knot. Now tie a square knot with the two far right cords (purple and pink).

Step #4: Repeat Step 2 and create a further central knot.

Step #5: Continue to alternate between the two steps until the required length is reached.

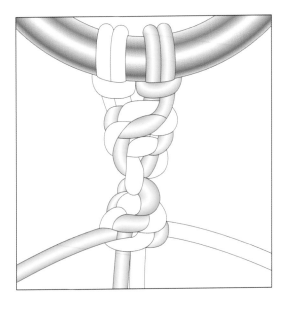

HALF KNOT

Use the first two steps of the square knot. Doing this over and over creates a spiral.

STRAIGHT DOUBLE HALF HITCH

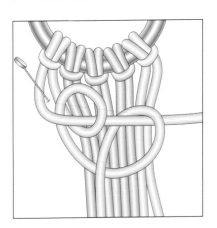 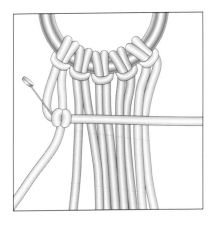 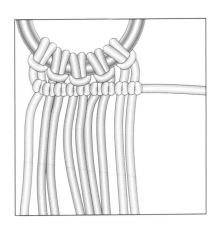

Step #1: A half hitch is a simple overhand knot. The working end is brought over and under the carrier cord, the carrier cord being the cord that carries the knots. Insert a pin between the two cords to give something to pull against. Tie two half hitch knots around the far left carrier cord.

Step #2: Pull the knot tight while holding the carrier cord horizontally straight.

Step #3: Repeat the same process along all the cords, tying two half hitch knits with each cord in turn to create a complete row using the same carrier cord.

KNOTS

DIAGONAL DOUBLE HALF HITCH

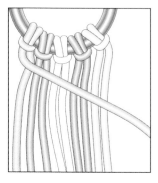 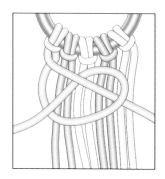

Step #1: Starting on the left-hand side, take the carrier cord and place it diagonally across all the cords, pin in place.

Step #2: Take the second cord and tie two half hitch knots and gently tighten.

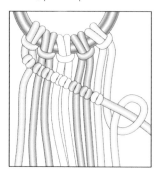 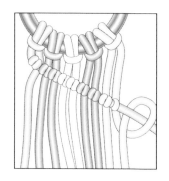 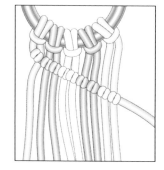

Step #3: Repeat along the line until the diagonal double hitch has been formed from left to right.

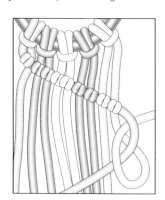 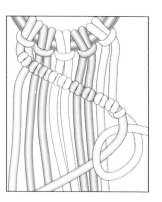 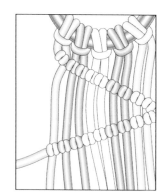

Step #4: Working now from right to left, repeat the steps above finishing with the pink thread back on the opposite side secured with two half hitch knots.

The completed double half hitch should look like this.

HIPPY ANKLET

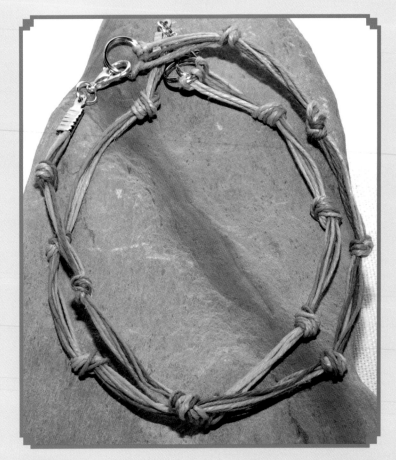

Materials needed

Three pieces of cord in different colors,
each measuring around 100 inches (2.5m) long
One 10mm split ring
One end clasp
One 6mm jump ring
One lobster clasp

Knots used: Overhand knot, larks head knot

H1PPY ANKLET

Before beginning, measure your ankle as the anklet needs to fit properly. I have used 9 inches (23cm) as a guide: adjust the cord length accordingly.

STEP #1 Fold the cords in half, and attach each to the split ring using a larks head knot.

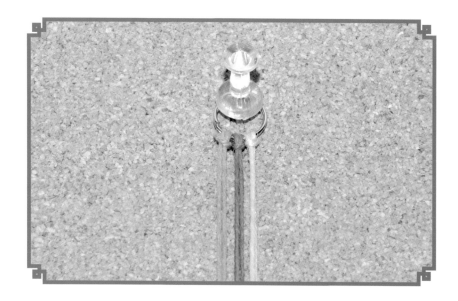

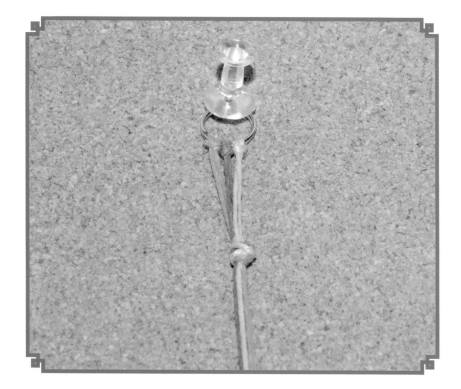

STEP #2 Leaving a gap of approximately 1 inch (2.5cm), take all of the cords and tie them together using an overhand knot.

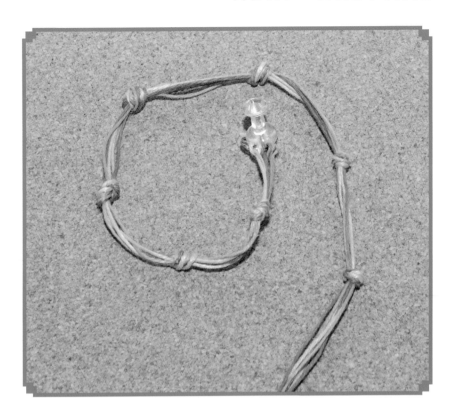

STEP #3 Continue to form a series of overhand knots as in Step #2, spacing them out evenly until your work measures around 9 inches (23cm) long or the required length.

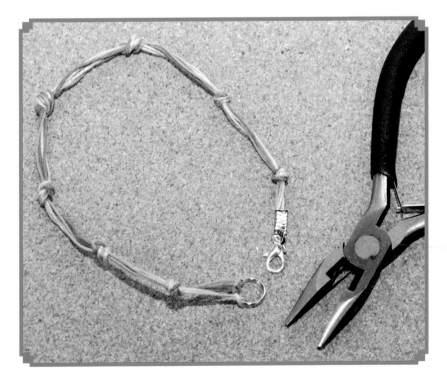

STEP #4 Snip off the excess cords and attach the end clasp, jump ring, and lobster clasp.

MULTI-STRANDED
SQUARE KNOT BRACELET

Materials needed

Three pairs of cord in different colors (A, B, C), each cord measuring around 120 inches (3m) long
One 10mm split ring
One end clasp
One 6mm jump ring
One lobster clasp

Required Knots: Square knot, larks head knot

MULTI-STRANDED SQUARE KNOT BRACELET

Begin by measuring your wrist. This will be the length the finished piece needs to be. I have worked to 6 inches (15cm) in total, but adjust this to fit your wrist. Remember to increase the length of cord if you want it to be longer.

STEP #1 Fold the color A cords in half, and attach each to the split ring using a larks head knot.

STEP #2 Form a series of square knots until the work measures around 6 inches (15cm) long.

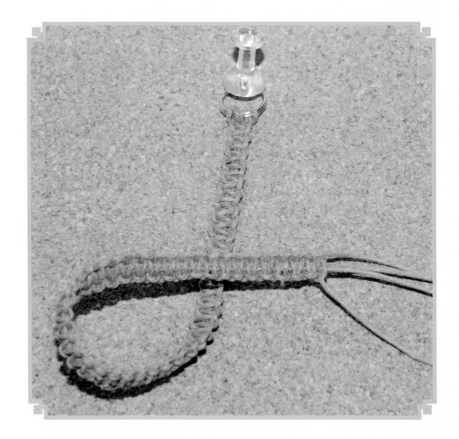

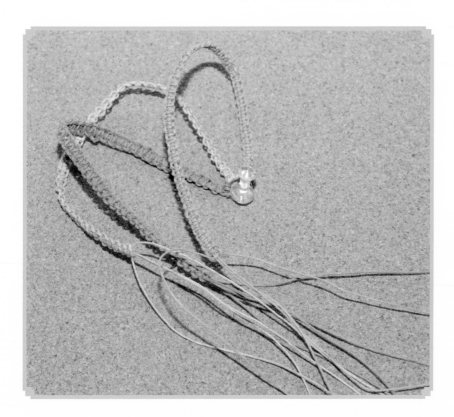

STEP #3 Repeat Steps #1 and #2 with the color B cords and then with color C.

STEP #4 Snip off the excess cords and attach the end clasp, jump ring, and lobster clasp.

SEA GLASS KEY FOB

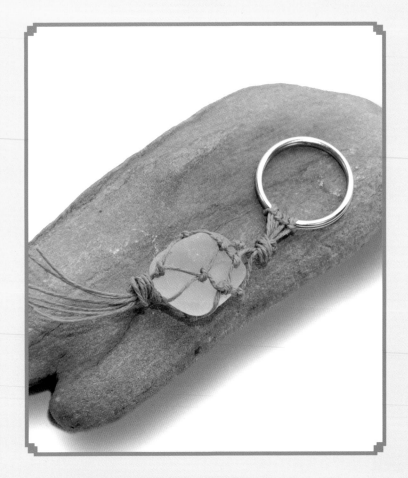

Materials needed

Four pieces of hemp cord, each measuring around 25 inches (63.5cm) long
One 30mm key ring
One piece of sea glass

Required Knots: Larks head knot, overhand knot

SEA GLASS KEY FOB

STEP #1 Fold the hemp cords in half, and attach each to the key ring using a larks head knot.

STEP #2 Gather all of the cords together to create one central strand using an overhand knot.

STEP #3 Divide the cords into twos, and then tie each set together using an overhand knot.

STEP #4 Continue to pair off: tie each two cords and begin to form a diamond shape.

STEP #5 Using the method shown in Steps #3 and #4, extend the shape down sufficiently to create a bag large enough to hold your piece of sea glass snugly.

STEP #6 Using all of the cords, perform a final overhand knot and pull tight. Trim off excess cords leaving a tail of approximately 1 inch (2.5cm).

SEA TURTLE SPIRAL BRACELET

Materials needed

Two pieces of hemp cord,
each measuring around 60 inches (152cm) long
One 10mm split ring
One charm bale

One end clasp
One 6mm jump ring
One lobster clasp

Required Knots: Half knot, larks head knot

SEA TURTLE SPIRAL BRACELET

Begin by measuring your wrist. This will be the length of the finished piece. I have worked to 6 inches (15cm), but adjust this to fit your wrist. Remember to increase the length of cord if you want it to be longer!

STEP #1 Fold the cords in half, and attach each to the split ring using a larks head knot.

STEP #2 Form a series of half knots creating a spiral until the work measures around 3 inches (7.5cm) long or your desired length.

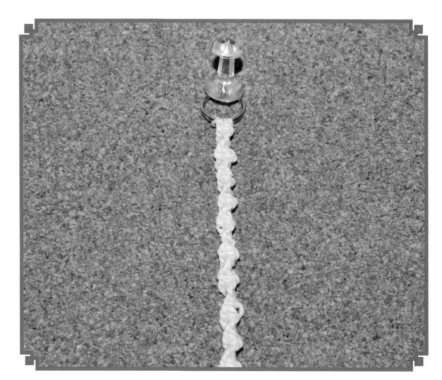

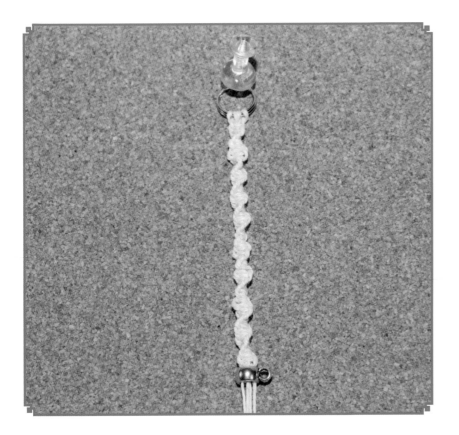

STEP #3 Thread all of the cords through the charm bale.

STEP #4 Continue to form half knots until the work measures around 6 inches (15cm) long, then snip off the excess cords. Attach the end clasp, jump ring, and lobster clasp, then add the charm to the bale using the 10mm jump ring.

SHELL CLUSTER NECKLACE

Materials needed

Two pieces of hemp cord,
each measuring around 180 inches (4.6m) long
One 10mm split ring
28 shell beads

One end clasp
One 6mm jump ring
One lobster clasp

Required Knots: Overhand knot, larks head knot

SHELL CLUSTER NECKLACE

STEP #1 Fold the cords in half, and attach each to the split ring using a larks head knot.

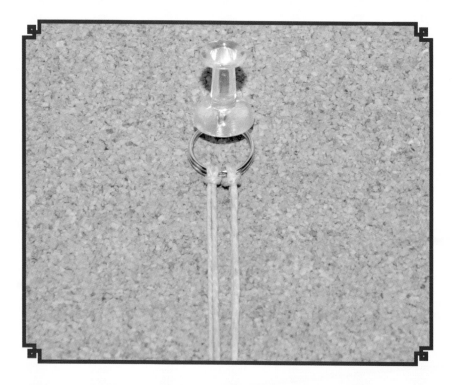

STEP #2 Using all of the cords, tie one overhand knot approximately 1 inch (2.5cm) down from the split ring.

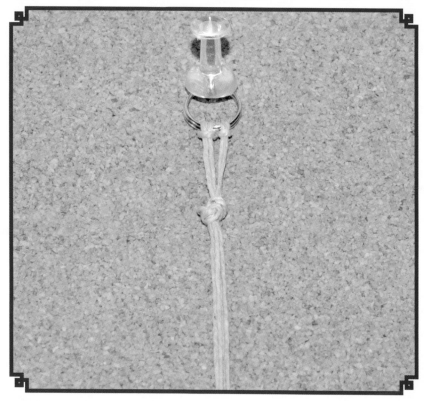

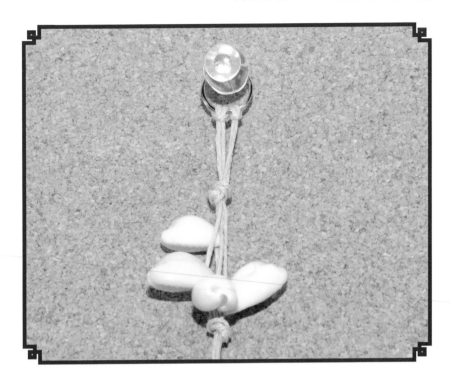

STEP #3 Thread a shell bead onto each cord, and then form an overhand knot with all of the cords.

STEP #4 Repeat Steps #2 and #3 leaving a 1½ inch gap (4cm) between each shell cluster until the work measures about 20 inches (50cm) long.

STEP #5 Snip off the excess cords and attach an end clasp, jump ring, and lobster clasp.

MULTI-STRANDED
BEACH-IN-A-BOTTLE NECKLACE

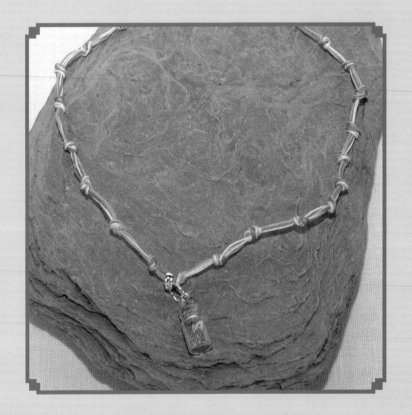

Materials needed

Three pieces of hemp cord in different colors, each measuring around 120 inches (3m) long
One 10mm split ring
One charm bale
One end clasp

One 6mm jump ring
One lobster clasp
One 10mm jump ring
A charm

Required Knots: Overhand knot, larks head knot

BEACH-IN-A-BOTTLE NECKLACE

STEP #1 Fold the cords in half, and attach each to the split ring using an overhand knot.

STEP #2 Tie all of the cords together using an overhand knot.

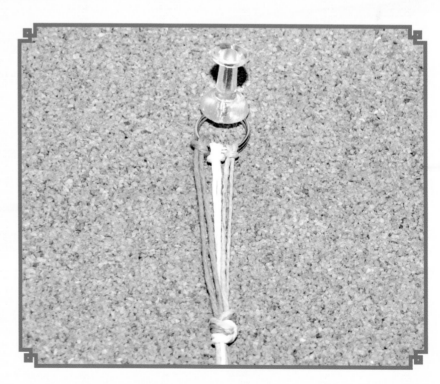

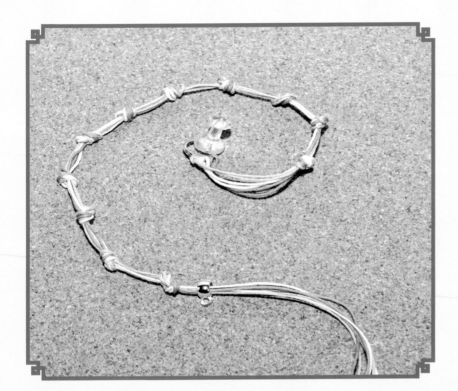

STEP #3 Continue to tie a series of overhand knots as in Step 2 until the work measures about 9 inches (23cm) long. Leave approximately 1 inch (2.5cm) between each overhand knot. Thread all the cords through the charm bale.

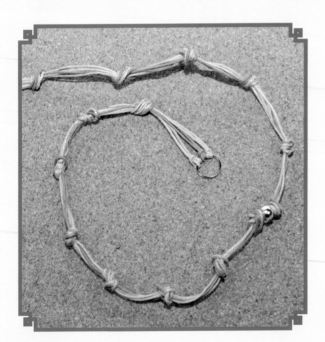

STEP #4 Tie an overhand knot close to the charm bale to secure it firmly.

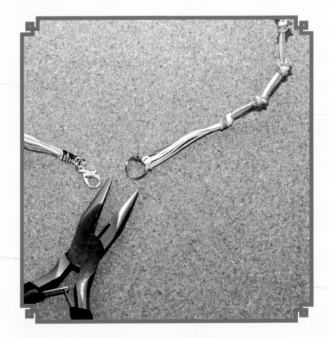

STEP #5 Attach the bale and finish off. Attach the bottle charm to the charm bale.

BEACH BABE HEADBAND

Materials needed

Three pairs of hemp cord in different colors (A, B, C), each piece measuring about 120 inches (3m) long
One 10mm split ring
One piece of elastic around 9 inches (23cm) long and 0.5 inches (1.25cm) wide
Sewing needle
White sewing thread
Safety pin

Required Knots: Square knot, larks head knot

BEACH BABE HEADBAND

The headband can be made to any size. If you prefer to have more band and less elastic, then use a longer length of cord for each section of the headband. Use a measuring tape and keep knotting until you reach the required length.

STEP #1 Fold the two color A cords in half, and attach each to the split ring using a larks head knot.

STEP #2 Form a series of square knots until the work measures around 12 inches (30cm) long or the required length.

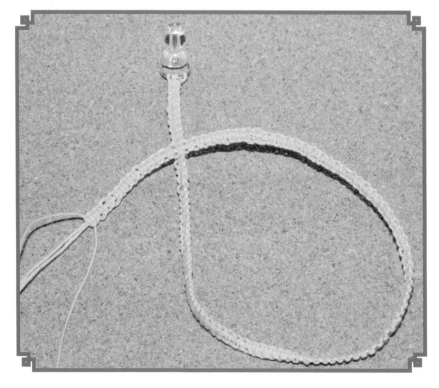

STEP #3 Repeat Steps #1 and #2 with color B cords, and then again with color C.

STEP #4 Make a braid with all of the cords by passing one outside strand across the center cord and then pass the other one across the center cord to form a braid or plait. Repeat, alternating one side and then the other. Repeat again. Continue to the end and pin securely to hold in place.

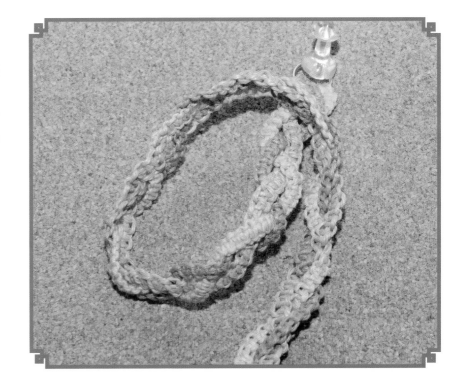

STEP #5 Measure the length of elastic required to ensure a comfortable fit for the headband and cut to the right length. Snip off the excess cords from the braid. Then, with a needle and thread, secure the braid so that it stays twisted and in place. Stitch each end of the work firmly to the elastic, trying to be as neat as possible.

STEP #6 The headband is now complete.

ANCHOR FRIENDSHIP BRACELET

Materials needed

Four pieces of hemp cord, each measuring around 30 inches (76cm) long
One anchor charm
100 size 11 silver seed beads
Two end clasps
One 6mm jump ring
One lobster clasp

Knots used: Larks head knot, square knot

ANCHOR FRIENDSHIP BRACELET

Begin by measuring your wrist. This will be the length the finished piece needs to be. I have worked to 6 inches (15cm) in total, but adjust this to fit your wrist. Remember to increase the length of cord and number of beads if it needs to be longer.

STEP #1 Take two of the cords, fold each in half, and attach to the top of the anchor using a larks head knot.

STEP #2 Form one square knot.

STEP #3 Thread a bead onto each of the two outer cords.

43

STEP #4 Continue to work Steps 2 and 3 until the work measures about 3 inches (7.5cm) long.

STEP #5 Attach the other two cords to the other end of the anchor using a larks head knot and repeat Steps 2–4.

STEP #6 Trim off excess cords and attach an end clasp to each end of the bracelet along with a jump ring and lobster clasp.

BEACH GYPSY NECKLACE

Materials needed

Four pieces of hemp cord,
each measuring about 100 inches (2.5m) long
One 10mm split ring
A wide selection of beads
One end clasp
One 6mm jump ring
One lobster clasp

Knots used: Overhand knot, larks head knot

BEACH GYPSY NECKLACE

This is a fun necklace to make, so really go to town with the choice of beads. Try using a mixture of focal beads and seed beads as this will make the bolder beads really stand out.

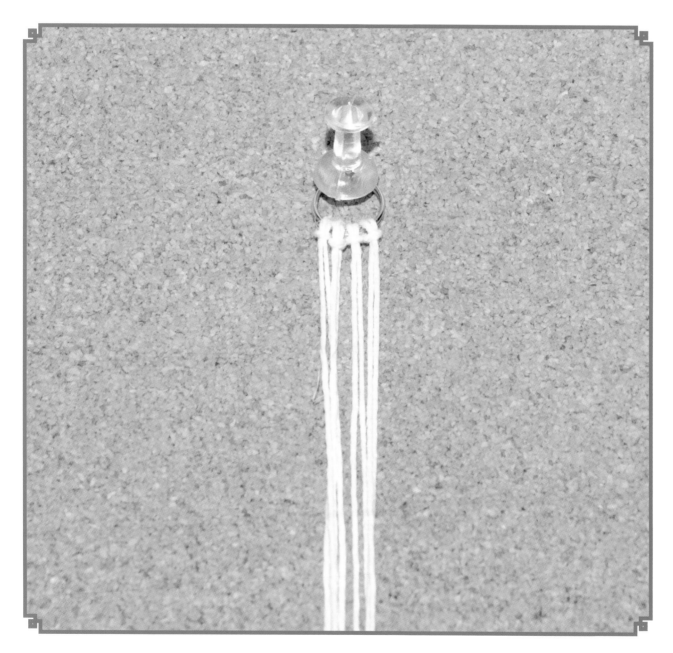

STEP #1 Fold the cords in half, and attach each to the split ring using a larks head knot.

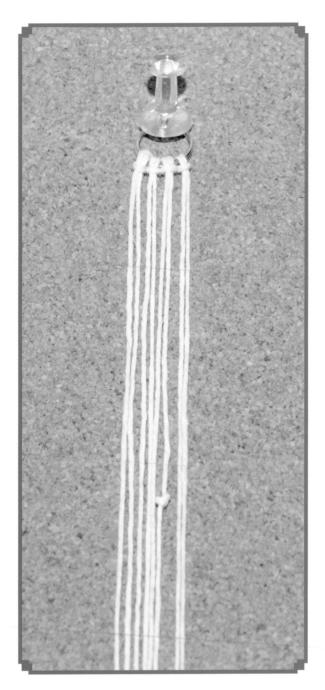

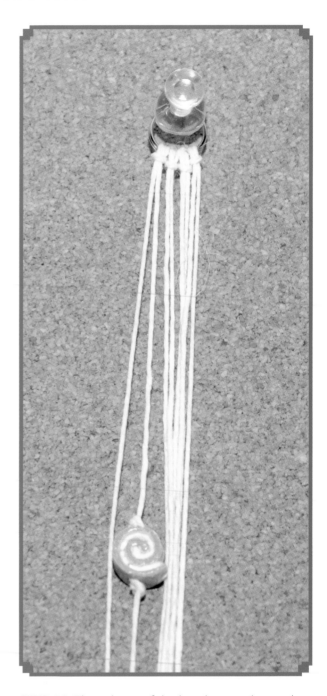

STEP #2 Take one of the cords and form an overhand knot.

STEP #3 Thread one of the beads onto the cord with the overhand knot, and then form another overhand knot to secure the bead in place.

BEACH GYPSY NECKLACE

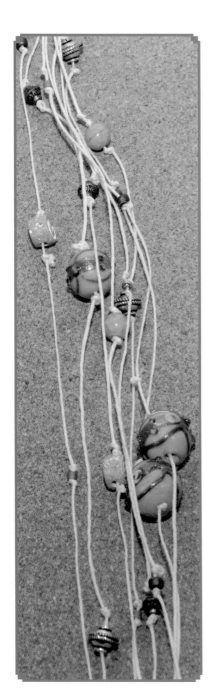

STEP #4 Continue to work Steps #2 and #3 over all of the cords, adding the knots and beads in random fashion until the work measures around 20 inches (50cm) long. Be creative. Use many types of bead and make it fun and funky.

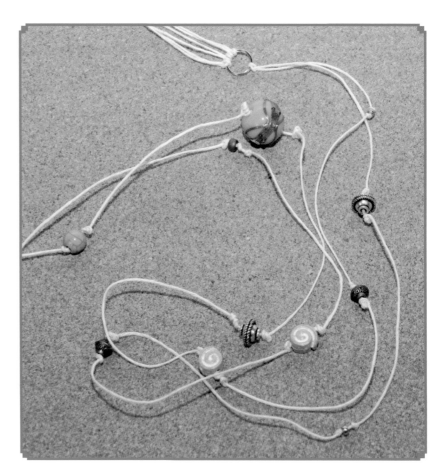

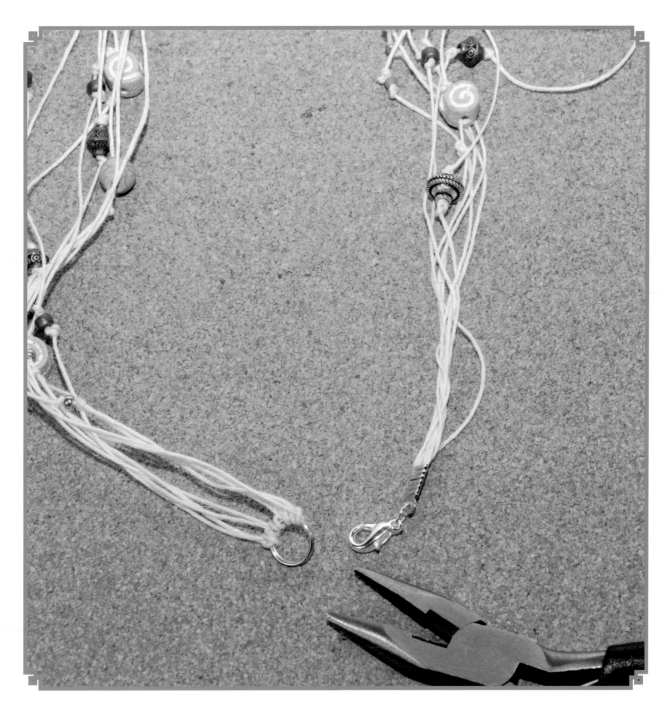

STEP #5 Snip off the excess cords and attach the end clasp, jump ring, and lobster clasp.

HEMP WRAP ANKLET

Materials needed

Two pieces of hemp cord, each measuring around 180 inches (4.57m) long
One charm bale
One 10mm split ring
11 8mm turquoise beads
10 size 6 silver beads

One end clasp
One 6mm jump ring
One lobster clasp
One 10mm jump ring
One charm

Required Knots: Larks head knot, square knot

52

HEMP WRAP ANKLET

Before beginning, wrap a strand of hemp around your ankle—this will ensure you end up with the correct length. Measure two-thirds of this and then add the charm bale. Continue to knot, following the instructions below, until you reach the full measurement required.

STEP #1 Fold the hemp cords in half, and attach each to the split ring using a larks head knot.

STEP #2 Form six square knots.

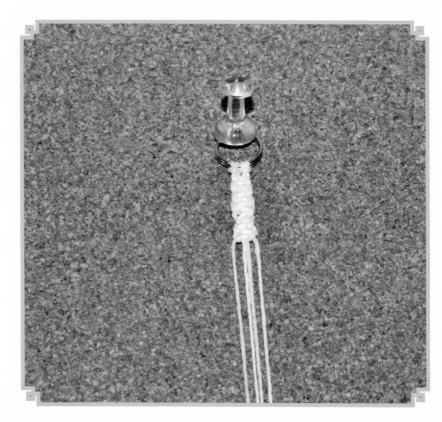

STEP #3 Thread one of the beads through the two inner cords.

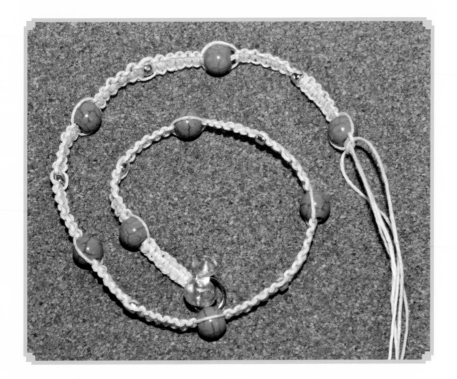

STEP #4 Continue to repeat Steps #2 and #3, alternating the beads, until the work measures 14 inches (35cm) long—or long enough to wrap around your ankle one and a half times.

STEP #5 Thread all of the cords through the charm bale, then make two more square knots. Next thread a turquoise bead through the two inner cords.

STEP #6 Continue to work Steps #2 and #3 as before until the work measures around 19 inches (48cm) long—the anklet should now be long enough to wrap around your ankle twice. If the length is not sufficient, continue Steps 2 and 3 until it's long enough. Finish the work on a row of square knots. Snip off the excess cord and attach the end clasp, jump ring, and lobster clasp. Finally, attach the charm to the charm bale with the 10mm jump ring.

SPIRAL EARRINGS

Materials needed

Four pieces of hemp cord, each measuring around 24 inches (61cm) long
Two 10mm split rings or closed jump rings
Around 100 size 6 silver seed beads
Two size 6 or size 8 silver barrel focal beads
Two ear wires

Required Knots: Half knot, larks head knot

SP1RAL EARR1NGS

STEP #1 Fold two of the hemp cords in half, and attach each to the split ring using a larks head knot.

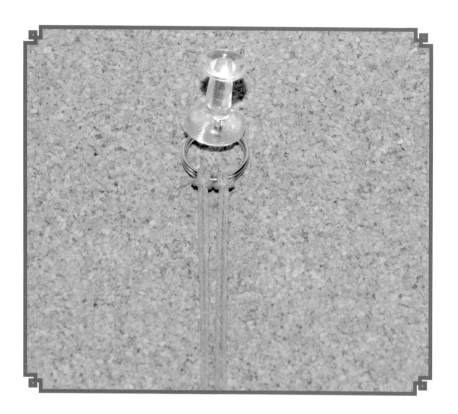

STEP #2 Form a half knot.

STEP #3 Thread one bead each side onto the two outer cords.

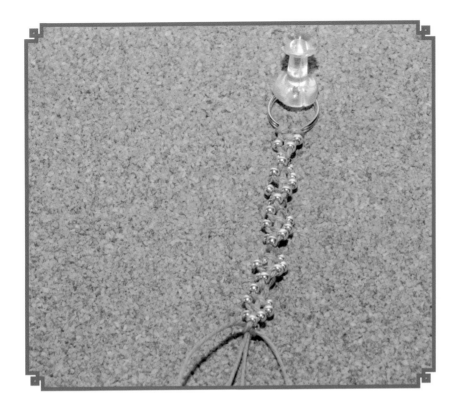

STEP #4 Repeat Steps #2 and #3 forming a spiral. Continue knotting until the work measures approximately 1.75 inches (4.5cm).

STEP #5 Thread all of the cords though a focal bead, and then form one overhand knot. Snip off the excess cords leaving a short tail. Repeat the process for earring number two, and then attach an ear wire to each earring.

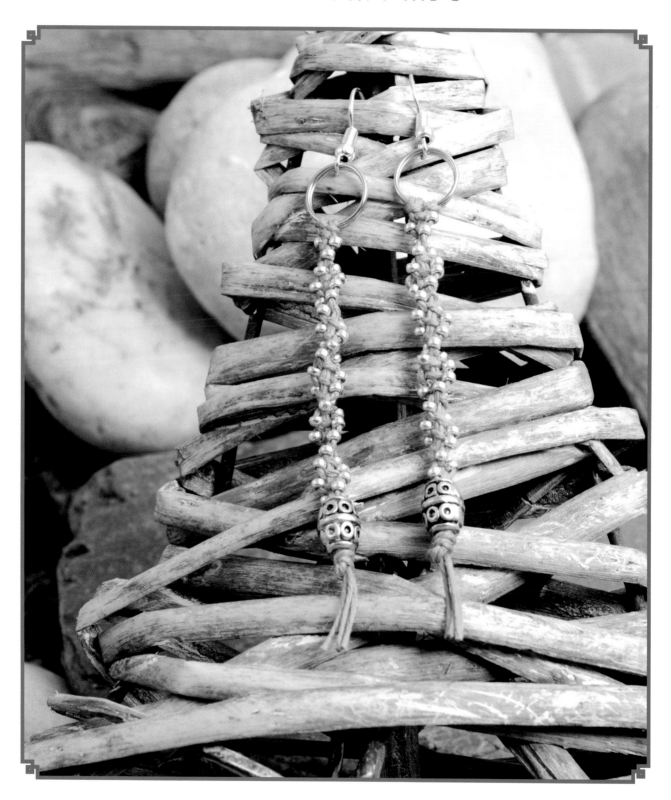

SHELL ANKLET

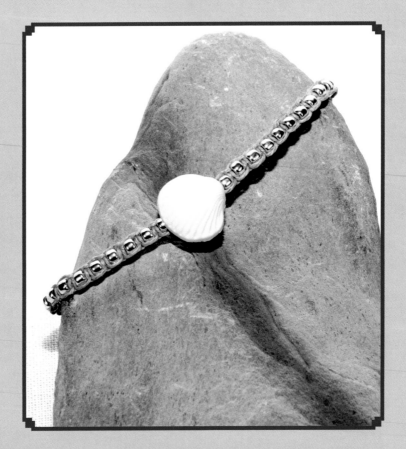

Materials needed

Two pieces of hemp cord, each measuring around 120 inches (3m) long
One 10mm split ring
Around 30 size 6 seed beads
One shell button with shank
One end clasp
One 10mm jump ring
One lobster clasp

Required Knots: Square knot, larks head knot

SHELL ANKLET

Before beginning, measure your ankle. Divide this measurement by two. The resulting figure identifies how long each half of your work should be. I have used 8 inches (20cm) as a guide.

STEP #1 Fold the hemp cords in half, and attach each to the split ring using a larks head knot.

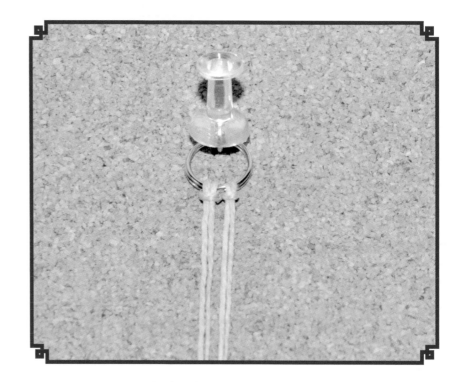

STEP #2 Form one square knot.

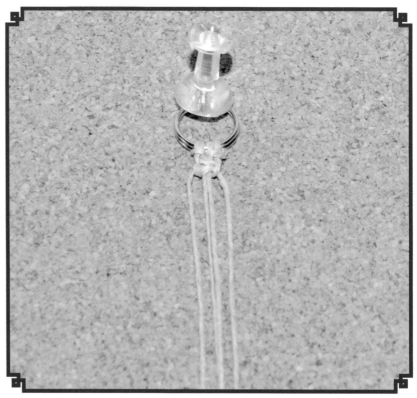

STEP #3 Thread the two inner cords through one of the beads.

STEP #4 Repeat Steps #2 and #3 until the work measures around 4 inches (10cm) long, then thread all of the cords though the button.

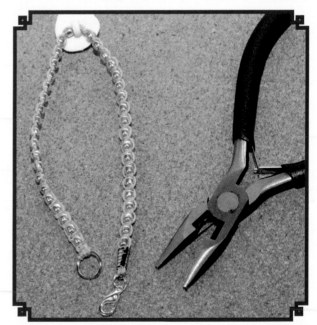

STEP #5 Continue to repeat Steps #2 and #3 until the work measures around 9 inches (23cm) long, then snip off the excess cords and attach end clasp, jump ring, and lobster clasp.

KNOTTED SEA GLASS BRACELET

Materials needed

Two pieces of hemp cord, each measuring about 60 inches (1.5m) long
One 10mm split ring
Nine pieces of center-drilled sea glass or large frosted-glass beads
One end clasp
One 6mm jump ring
One lobster clasp

Required Knots: Half knot, overhand knot, larks head knot

KNOTTED SEA GLASS BRACELET

Begin by measuring your wrist. This will be the length of the finished piece. I have worked to 6 inches (15cm) for the total length, but adjust this to fit your wrist. Remember to increase the number of beads and length of cord if you want it to be longer.

STEP #1 Fold the cords in half, and attach each to the split ring using a larks head knot.

STEP #2 Form a series of half knots to create a spiral and keep knotting until the work measures around 1 inch (2.5cm) in length.

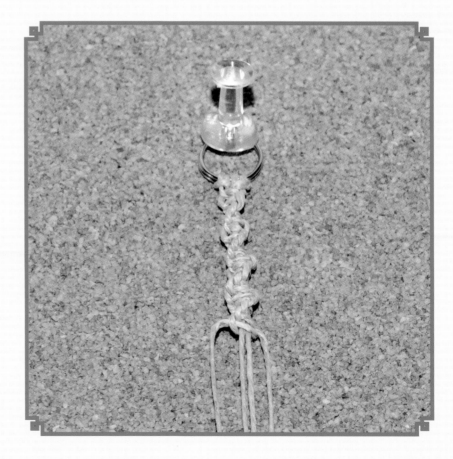

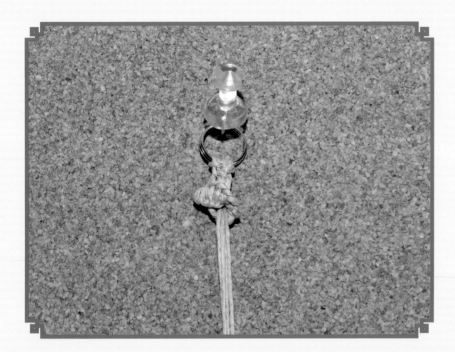

STEP #3 Using all of the cord form an overhand knot *over* the series of half knots.

STEP #4 Thread all of the cords through one piece of pre-drilled sea glass and then repeat Step #2 thru Step #3 until the work measures around 6 inches (15cm) long (or the desired length). Snip off the excess cords and attach the end clasp, jump ring, and lobster clasp.

TASSELS AND BEADS EARRINGS

Materials needed

Eight pieces of hemp cord,
each 24 inches (61cm) long
Two ear wires
Two split rings

Two 6mm seed beads
10 8mm seed beads of color A
10 8mm seed beads of color B
12 8mm seed beads of color C

Required Knots: Double half hitch knot, overhand knot, larks head knot

TASSELS AND BEADS EARRINGS

Take some cord with you when you go to the store to be certain that the hole in the 6mm seed beads is large enough to comfortably fit two cords.

STEP #1 Fold the cords in half, and attach each to the split ring using a larks head knot.

STEP #2 Using the first four cords on the left, and starting with the outermost cord, form a row of diagonal double half hitch knots.

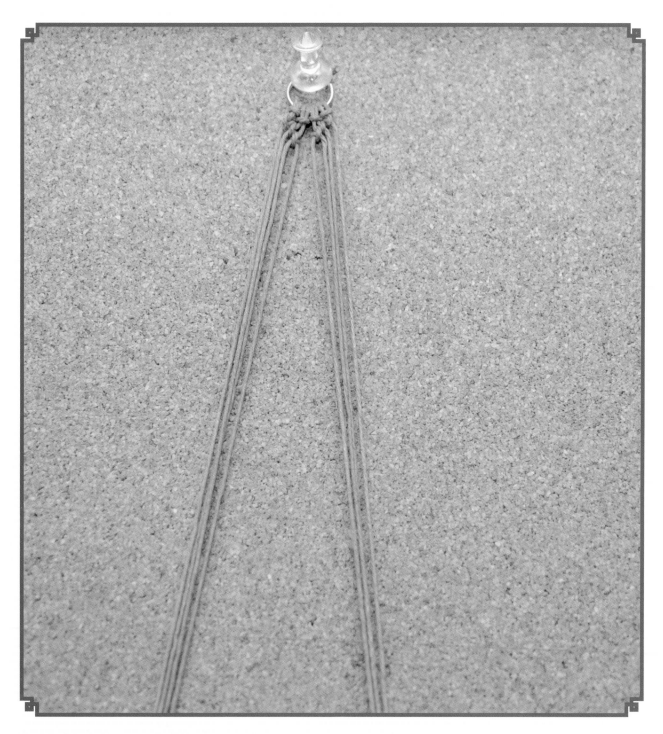

STEP #3 Repeat Step #2 with the cords on the right, working this time
from right to left.

STEP #4 Thread the two central cords through one of the size 6mm seed beads.

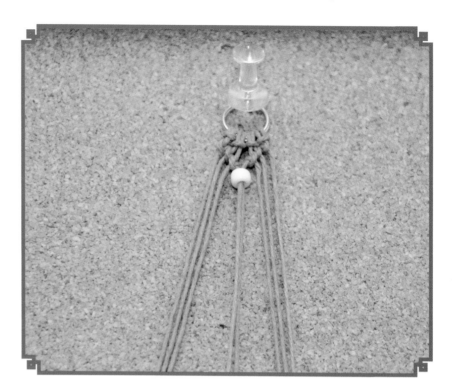

STEP #5 Thread three size 8mm seed beads onto the cord to the right of the two central cords.

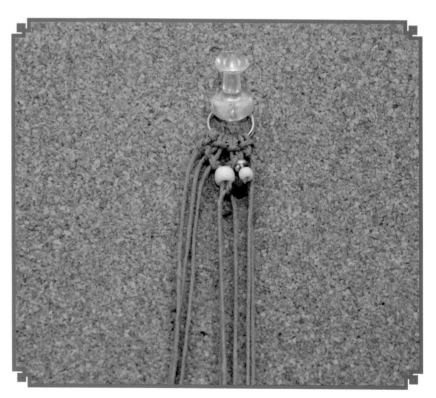

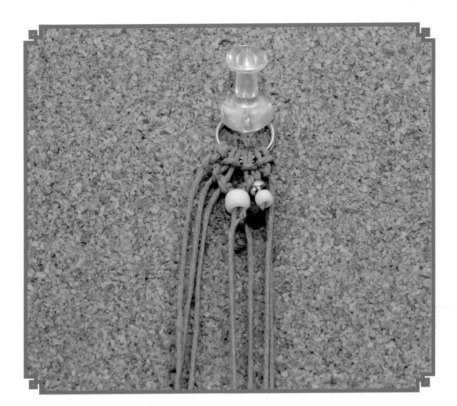

STEP #6 Wrap the cord with the three beads attached around the cord to the left (which has the size 6 seed bead on it) and form one double half hitch knot working left to right.

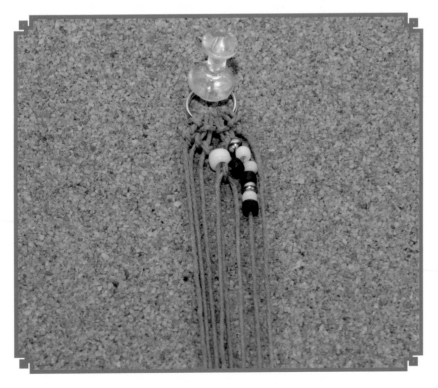

STEP #7 Thread five seed beads on to the next cord on the right.

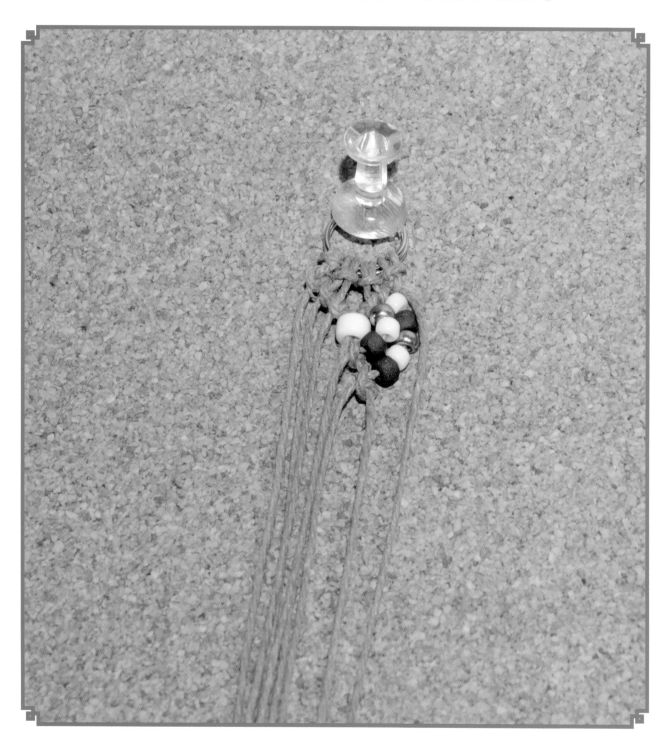

STEP #8 Wrap the cord with five beads attached around the cord to the left using a double half hitch knot as in Step #6.

STEP #9 Thread seven seed beads onto the final outside cord on the right.

STEP #10 Wrap the cord with seven beads attached around the cord to the left using a double half hitch knot.

STEP #11 Repeat Step #4 thru Step #10 with the cords on the left, but reversing the directions.

STEP #12 Form an overhand knot with all of the cords. Trim off the excess cords leaving around 1–2 inches (2.5–3cm) to create the tassel.

STEP #13 Attach the ear wire. Repeat the process once again for the second earring.

BAREFOOT SANDALS

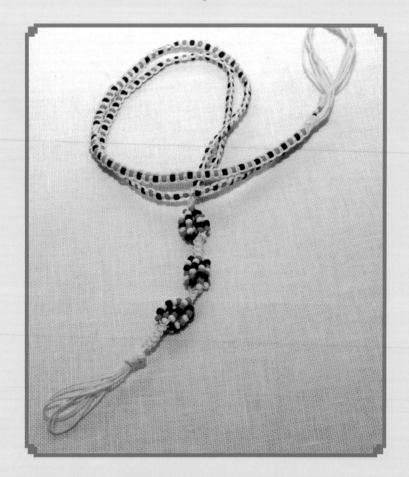

Materials needed

Each sandal requires:
Six pieces of hemp cord, each measuring 120 inches long
Around 100 size 8 seed beads in color A
Around 100 size 8 seed beads in color B
Around 50 size 8 seed beads in color C

Knots used: Square knot, overhand knot

BAREFOOT SANDALS

STEP #1 Fold the cords in half, and form an overhand knot around 1½ inches (4cm) down from the fold.

STEP #2 Form five square knots.

STEP #3 Thread six beads in random order onto every cord.

STEP #4 Form four square knots.

STEP #5 Repeat Steps #3 and #4 twice more.

STEP #6 Divide the cords into two sets of four, and then work one square knot with the first four cords.

STEP #7 Continue to work with the first set of cords and thread the two inner cords through one seed bead.

BAREFOOT SANDALS

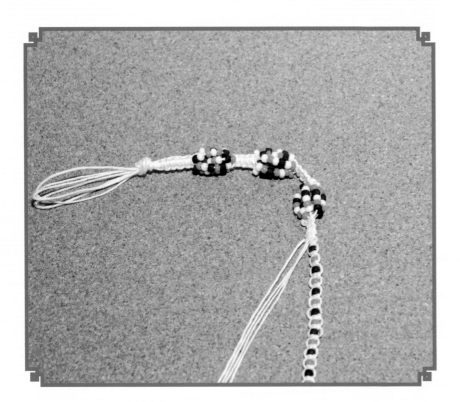

STEP #8 Continue to work Steps 6 and 7 until the work is long enough to wrap around your ankle from the front and around to the back again. (About 13 inches/33cm depending on your ankle.)

STEP #9 Repeat Step #6 thru Step #8 with the remaining four cords. The resulting two pieces are the sandal straps.

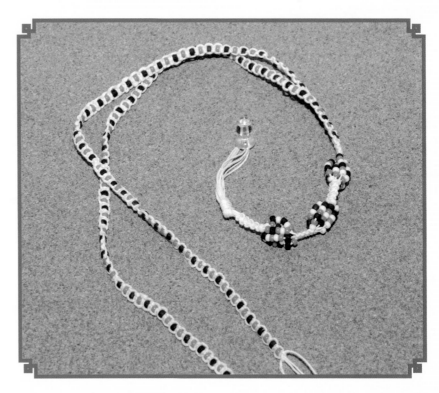

STEP #10 Tie an overhand knot at the end of the two new straps using all the cords.

STEP #11 To finish off both ends, leave around 8 inches (20cm), and then tie another overhand knot at the end of each end. Snip off the excess cords.

LARIAT NECKLACE

Materials needed

Two pieces of hemp cord,
each measuring around 100 inches (2.5m) long
One 10mm split ring
Six silver beads
Six silver barrel beads
One charm

One charm bale
One 10mm jump ring
One end clamp
One 6mm jump ring
One lobster clasp

Required Knots: Larks head knot, half knot

LAR1AT NECKLACE

STEP #1 Fold the hemp cords in half, and attach each to the split ring using a larks head knot.

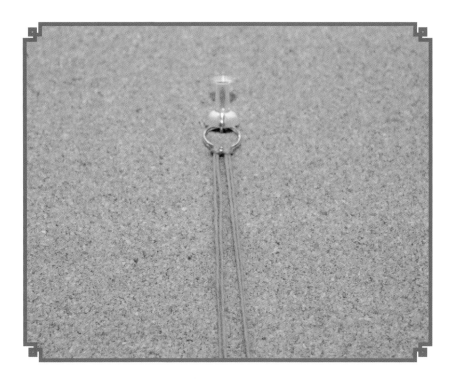

STEP #2 Form a series of half knots to create a spiral. Keep knotting until the work measures around 1 inch (2.5cm) long.

STEP #3 Thread all of the cords through one of the beads.

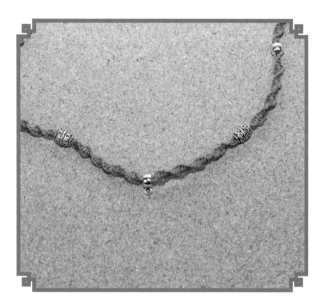

STEP #4 Continue to work in this way by repeating Steps 2# and #3 until the work measures around 10 inches (25cm) long or is half the desired length of the necklace.

STEP #5 Attach the charm bale, and then continue to work Step #2 thru Step #3 until the necklace has doubled in length.

STEP #6 Attach the charm to the pendant bale using the 10mm jump ring.

STEP #7 Trim off any excess cord and attach an end clamp, then add the jump ring and lobster clasp. Attach the charm to the pendant bale using the 10 mm jump ring.

SPIRALS AND LACE BRACELET

Materials needed

Six pieces of hemp cord, each measuring around 60 inches (1.5m) long
One 10mm split ring
One jump ring
One ribbon clamp
One lobster clasp

Required Knots: Larks head knot, half knot, double half hitch knot, and alternating square knot

SP1RALS AND LACE BRACELET

Begin by measuring your wrist. This will be the length the finished piece needs to be. I have worked to 6 inches (15cm) in total, but adjust this to fit your wrist. Remember to increase the length of cord if you want it to be longer.

STEP #1 Fold the cords in half, and attach each to the split ring using a larks head knot.

STEP #2 Using the first four cords on the left, form 12 half knots creating a spiral.

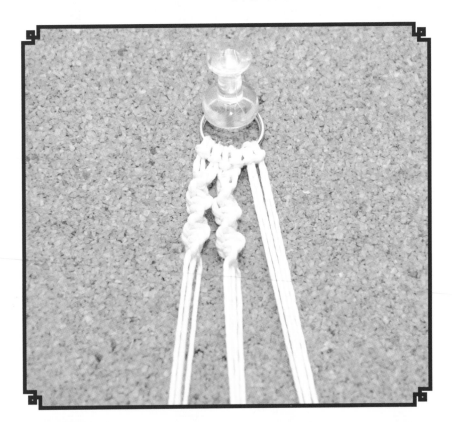

STEP #3 Repeat Step #2 using the four cords in the middle.

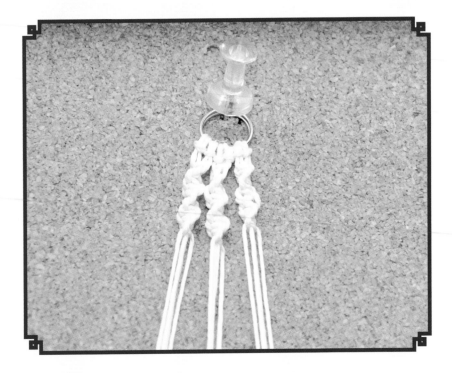

STEP #4 Repeat Step #2 using the first four cords on the right.

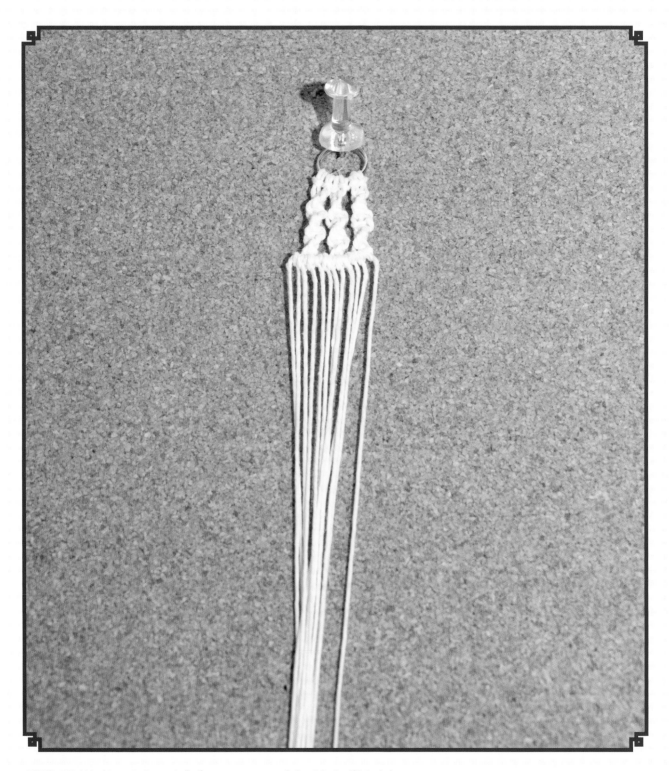

STEP #5 Working right to left, form one row of double half hitch knots.

STEP #6 Using the first four cords on the right, form one square knot.

STEP #7 Working right to left, use the next four cords to form a further square knot.

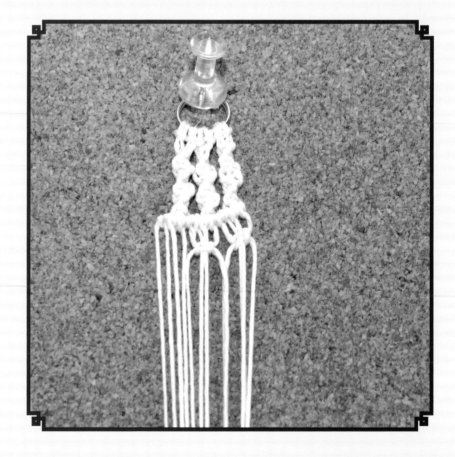

SPIRALS AND LACE BRACELET

STEP #8 Using the last four cords, form another square knot.

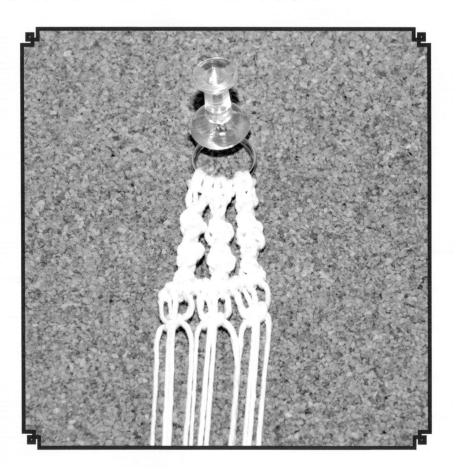

STEP #9 Working right to left, *omit* the first two cords, and using the following next four cords, form one square knot.

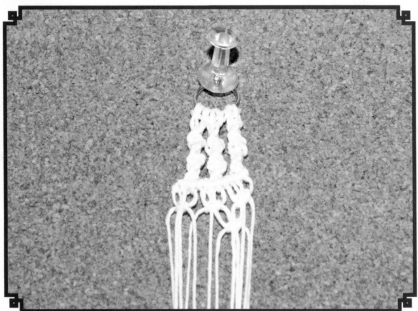

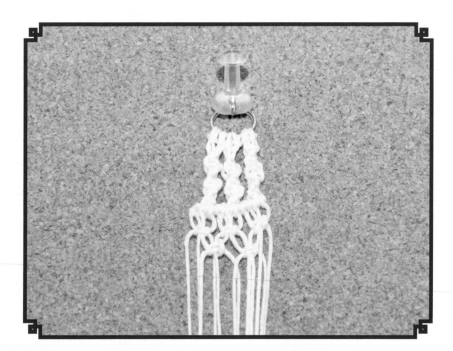

STEP #10 Using the next four cords, form another square knot.

STEP #11 Repeat Step #2 thru Step #10 until the work measures around 6 inches (15cm) long or the required length. Snip off the excess cords and attach a ribbon clamp, jump ring, and lobster clasp.

NATURAL HEMP CUFF

Materials needed

Seven pieces of hemp cord measuring about
30 inches (76cm) long
One 10mm split ring
64 size 8 seed beads color A

32 size 8 seed beads color B
One ribbon clamp
One 6mm jump ring
One lobster clasp

Required Knots: Double half hitch knot, larks head knot

NATURAL HEMP CUFF

Begin by measuring your wrist. This will be the length the finished piece needs to be. I have worked to 6 inches (15cm) in total, but adjust this to fit your wrist. Remember to increase the number of beads and length of cord if you want it to be longer.

STEP #1 Fold the cords in half, and attach each to the split ring using a larks head knot.

STEP #2 Using the first six cords on the left and, starting with the outermost cord, form a row of diagonal double half hitch knots.

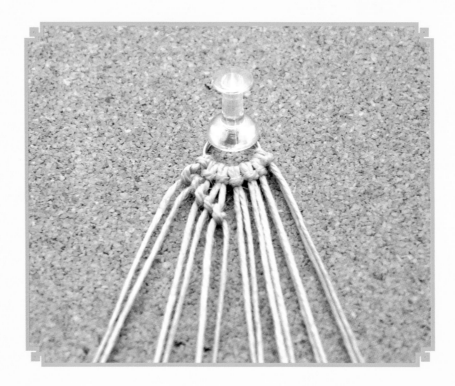

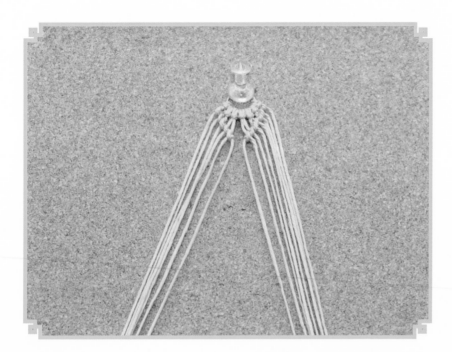

STEP #3 Repeat Step #2 with the cords on the right, this time working from right to left.

STEP #4 Using the two central cords, form one double half hitch knot. This joins the two sides together again.

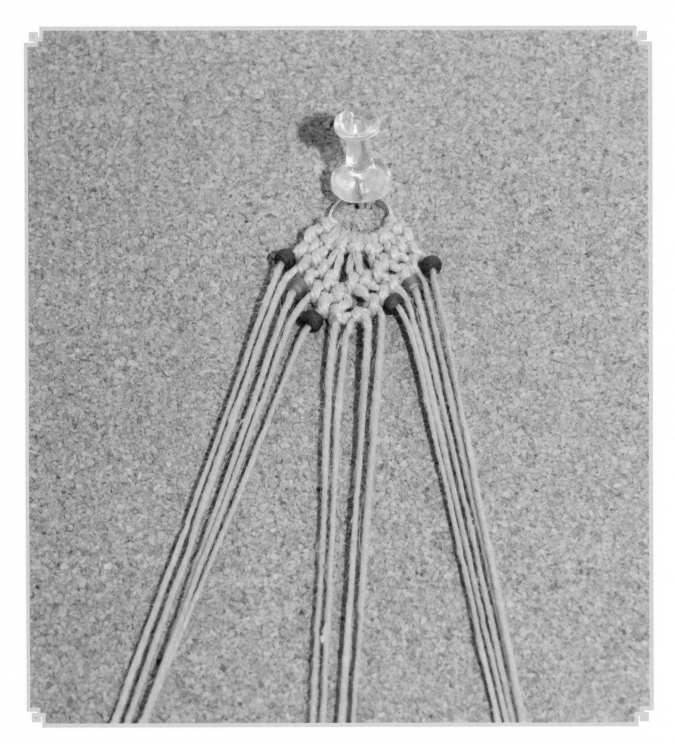

STEP #5 Starting with the two outer cords, thread a seed bead onto every other cord—but *omit* the four central cords.

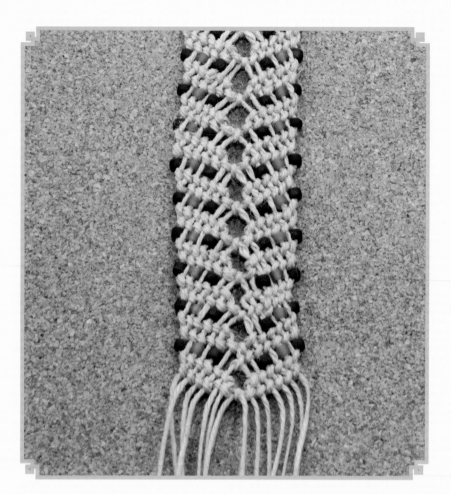

STEP #6 Repeat Step #2 thru Step #5 until the work measures around 6 inches (15cm) long or the required length.

STEP #7 Snip off the excess cords and attach a ribbon clamp, jump ring, and lobster clasp.

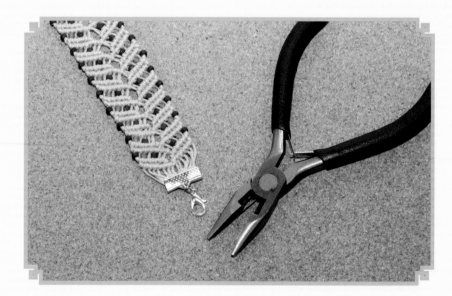

LACY ANCHOR BRACELET

Materials needed

Six pieces of hemp cord, each 60 inches (1.5m) long
Two 10mm split rings
One focal button
One end clamp

One 6mm jump ring
One lobster clasp

Required Knots: Double half hitch knot, overhand knot, larks head knot

LACY ANCHOR BRACELET

Before beginning, measure your wrist. Take the measurement and divide by two. This is how long each half of the work to the focal button should be. I have used 6 inches (15cm) as a guide. Make sure the buttonhole is large enough to thread 12 cords through.

STEP #1 Fold the cords in half, and attach each to the split ring using a larks head knot.

STEP #2 Using the first four cords on the left, form one square knot.

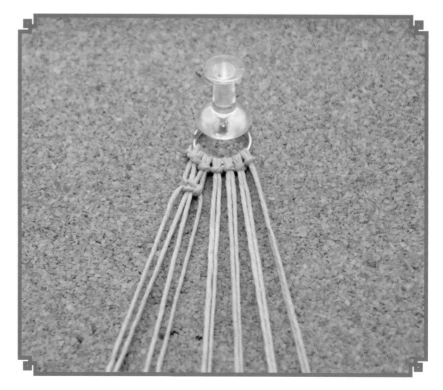

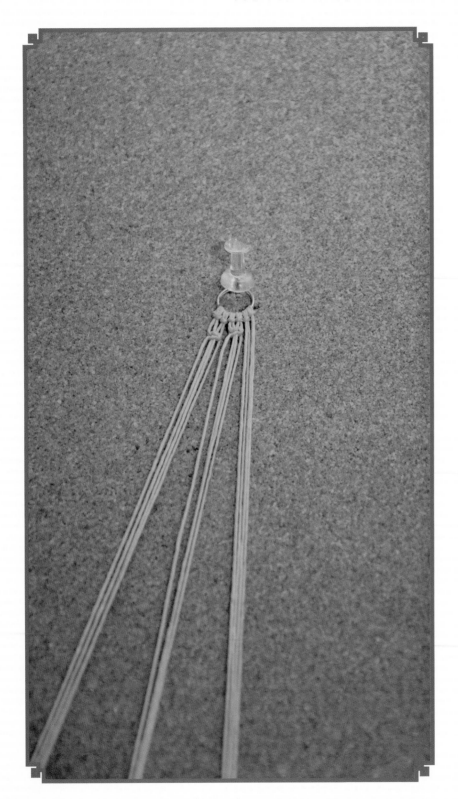

STEP #3 Using the four cords in the middle, form one square knot.

LACY ANCHOR BRACELET

STEP #4 Using the four cords on the right, form one square knot.

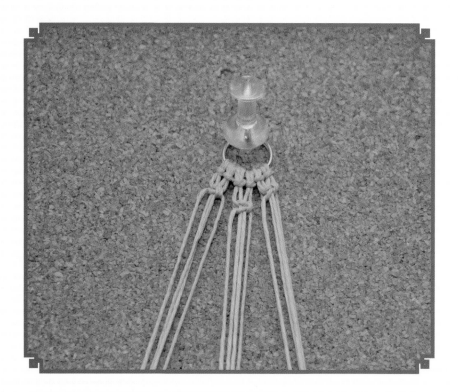

STEP #5 Working from right to left, leave the first two cords and then form one square knot with the remaining four cords.

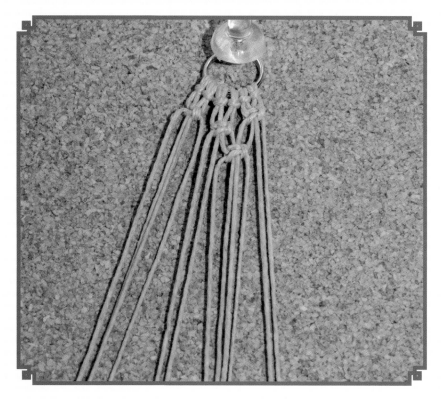

STEP #6 Using the following four cords, again working right to left, form a square knot.

STEP #7 Continue to work Step #2 thru Step #6 until the work measures about 3 inches (7.5cm) long.

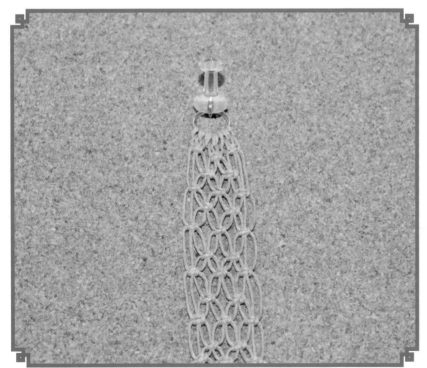

LACY ANCHOR BRACELET

STEP #8 Tie all of the cords together using an overhand knot.

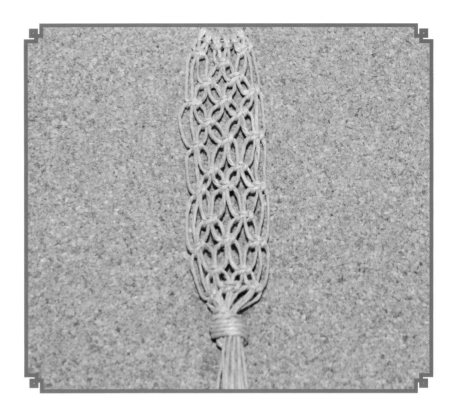

STEP #9 Thread all of the cords through your button.

STEP #10 Using all the knots again, tie another overhand knot next to the button.

STEP #11 Repeat Step #2 thru Step #6 until the work measures around 3 inches (15cm) long or the required length. Snip off the excess cords and attach an end clamp, jump ring, and lobster clasp.

BOHO BEACH BRACELET

Materials needed

Four pieces of hemp cord,
each measuring about
60 inches (1.5m) long
One 10mm split ring
100 size 8 seed beads in color A

30 size 6 seed beads in color B
One ribbon end clasp
One lobster clasp
Two jump rings

Knots used: Double half hitch knot, larks head knot

BOHO BEACH BRACELET

Begin by measuring your wrist. This will be the length the finished piece needs to be. I have worked to 6 inches (15cm) in total, but adjust this to fit your wrist. Remember to increase the number of beads and length of cord if you want it to be longer.

STEP #1 Fold the cords in half, and attach each to the split ring using a larks head knot.

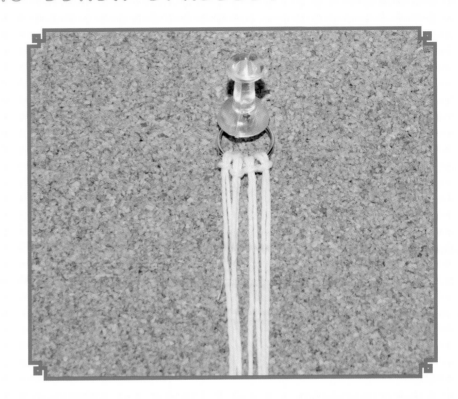

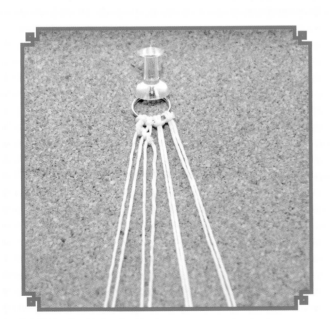

STEP #2 Using the first four cords on the left and starting with the outermost cord, form a row of diagonal double half hitch knots.

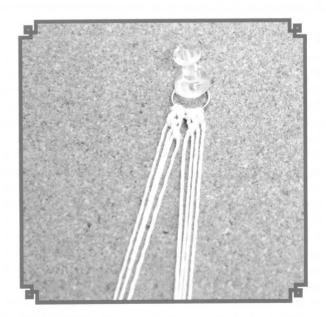

STEP #3 Using the first four cords on the right and starting with the outermost cord, form a row of diagonal double half hitch knots.

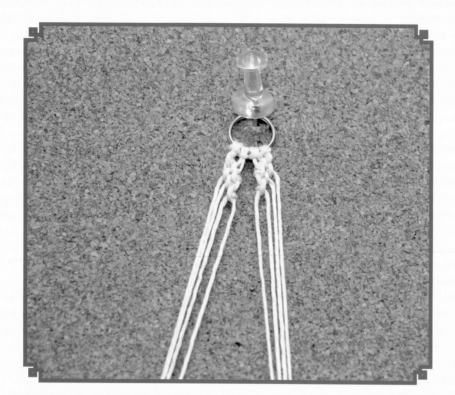

STEP #4 Repeat Steps #2 and #3 again.

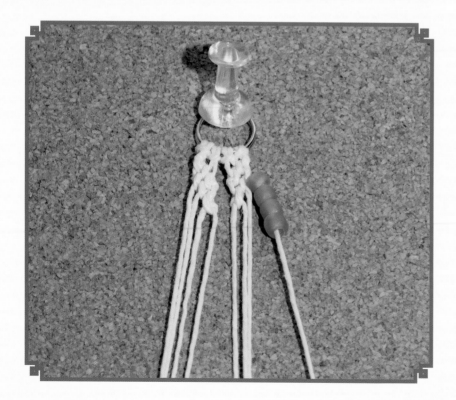

STEP #5 Thread four of the color A seed beads onto the first cord on the right.

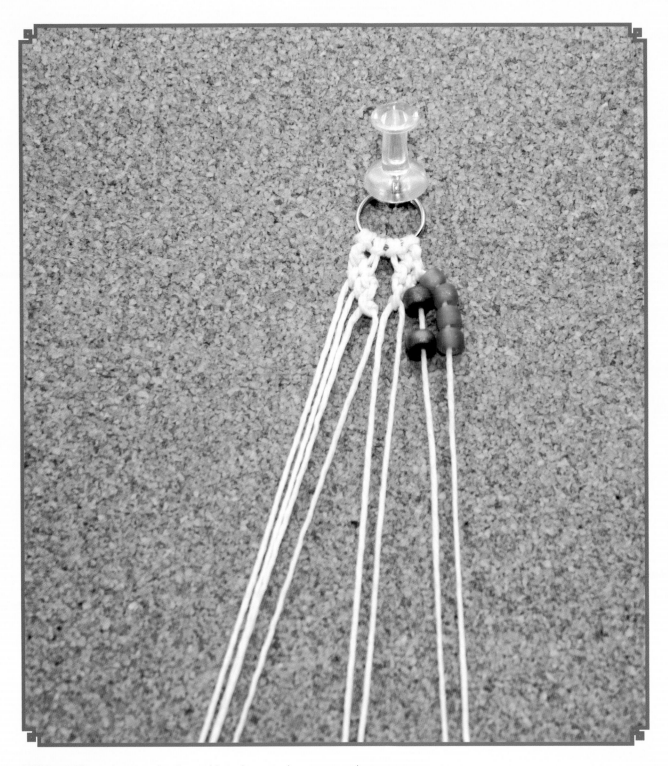

STEP #6 Thread two color B seed beads onto the next cord.

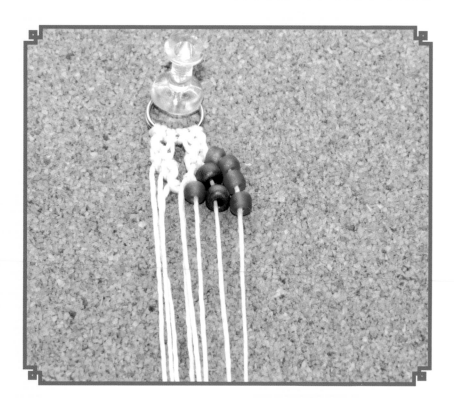

STEP #7 Thread one color A seed bead onto the next cord.

STEP #8 Using the cord fourth from the right and working from left to right, form a row of diagonal half hitch knots.

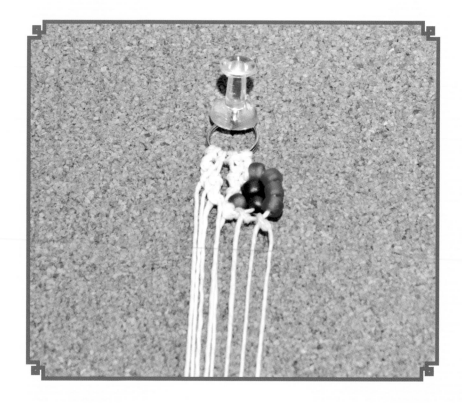

STEP #9 Repeat Steps #4 thru Step #8 using the cords on the left. The last row of diagonal half hitch knots are created using the fourth cord from the left and working from right to left.

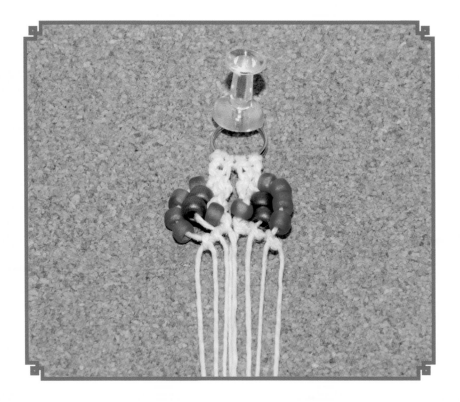

STEP #10 Form one row of double half hitch knots working left to right.

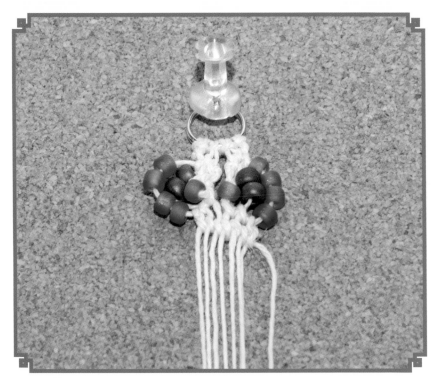

STEP #11 Divide the cords into pairs, and then thread each pair through a color A seed bead.

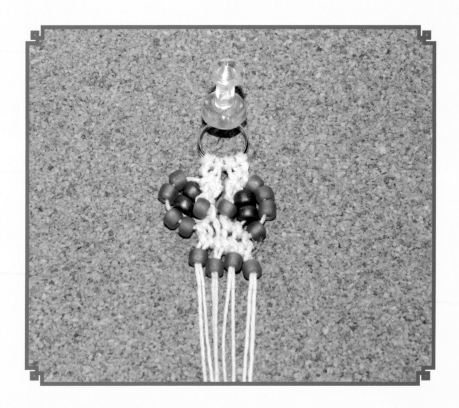

STEP #12 Continue to work Step #2 thru Step #11 until the work measures around 6 inches (15cm) or your required length. Snip off the excess cords and attach the ribbon end clasp, lobster clasp, and jump ring.

Dedicated to Robin and Lynzi and to celebrate the birth of my beautiful granddaughter Evie.